Contribitors

Anne Scottlin, MA, CPC
Sher J. Stultz
Gary Robinson
L.J. Ambrosio
Anna J Stewart
Chris Lau
JP McLean
Marina Koulouri
Raymond F. Klein
Rose Elaine
Sam Choi
Tshekedi Wallace
Valerie D. Johnson
Van Fleisher
Edward Willett
Charles Townsend
George Pallas
John Ingram Walker, MD
Charles Townsend
Dan E. Hendrickson
Mitzi Perdue
Eckhart Aurelius Hughes
Dana Sardano
Linnea Tanner
Craig W. Stanfill

Special thanks to:
Scott Hughes
Onlinebookclub.org

Review Tales

A Book Magazine For Indie Authors

COPYRIGHT © 2023
Review Tales Magazine
A Book Magazine for Indie Authors
This magazine may not be reproduced,
either in part or in its entirety, in any
form, by any means, without written
permission from the publisher, with the
exception of brief excerpts for purposes
of radio, television, or published reviews.
Although all possible means have been
taken to ensure the accuracy of the
material presented, Review Tales is not
liable for any misinterpretation,
misapplication or typographical errors.
All rights, including the right of translation,
are reserved.
Founder & Editor in Chief: S. Jeyran Main
Publisher: Review Tales Publishing &
Editing Services
Print & Distribution: IngramSparks
Cover Photo: Moldy vintages-10625835
Designs: Pexels
ISBN 978-1-988680-24-8 (Paperback)
ISBN 978-1-988680-25-5 (Digital)
www.jeyranmain.com
For all inquiries, please get in touch with us
directly.

A BOOK MAGAZINE FOR INDIE AUTHORS

REVIEW TALES

TABLE OF CONTENTS

Editor's Notes

Review Tales Magazine

We ring in the New Year with hope and a promise. We hope the holiday season has given you enjoyment and that 2023 is filled with much-needed love and success. We promise to bring an even more diverse and collectively improved magazine for our book lovers and authors.

With all the success that followed last year and the launch of Review Tales Magazine, I was not expecting such a wonderful reception. I always knew the writing community needed such a platform, and as I would converse with so many authors, I understood the value of its creation. However, what transpired was an overwhelming amount of support, love, and, ultimately, an inspirational outcome.

While I sit here and write for the first edition of this year's magazine, I want to let you all know that we plan to keep altering, innovating, and challenging magazine standards. We resolve to make resolutions as we go and purely write for you.

The winter 2023 issue is filled with the evolution of an author, the confessions of a sci-fi writer, and how an author has found freedom and truth through writing. We invite late bloomers to this wonderful world of inventiveness and all the inspired authors who write and use visual imagination in their books.

A lot can happen in a year, and between the good, the bad, and the ugly, this may seem like an understatement to most. As glasses are raised, and fireworks explode into the sky, it's important to recognize the special symbolism of the New Year.

Jeyran Main

Founder & Editor-in-chief
Review Tales Magazine - Publishing & Editing Services

Evolution of an Author
Anne Scottlin, MA, CPC

An author may not be made in a day. For most of us, becoming an author is a process, an evolution; it is the fulfillment and, ultimately, the culmination of our self-expression to the world. If writing is in your blood, you can't help but write and always will because it is part of expressing your joy for being alive. At least, that's how it is for me.

I may not have been born with a pen or keyboard in my hands, but I was a natural-born storyteller. My father was a great storyteller, too. I used to beg him to tell me more stories about the adventures and antics of his own childhood and life as bedtime stories. There were always more. And I loved them. Growing up, I wasn't allowed to have television, which may have helped my imagination run wild.

By age eight or nine, I was inventing fictional, continued stories that I would force my little brothers to sit and listen to, and eventually, any other poor kids I came across. I was always a big fan of serial stories to keep their attention and make them return. By age ten, I wrote my first play.

My serious writing journey began with a writing mentor and my senior-year English teacher in a tiny country high school. Thank you to all you passionate teachers out there who really care about your students and give them extra time. Mrs Peters affirmed my ability to create a story and to be persuasive. She wrote lots of margin notes on my papers that were pure gold. I will always be grateful for her encouragement and belief in me.

After that, my story journey took several detours, from a graduate degree in Medieval history, where I wrote an award-winning thesis on Medieval women writers, to writing screenplays and working as a Hollywood actress. My fascination with story and history culminated in my commitment to change our collective story in progress, to leave the world a better place than I found it.

After working as a professional in the industries of personal empowerment and growth mindset for over a decade, I saw how little time people seemed to find for emotional self-care. I decided to write a self-empowerment book that people could benefit from even if they only had a couple of minutes a day. My full-color book, Live for Joy, became an Amazon Best-Seller and a Winner of the Global Book Awards in 2022. I'm now on schedule to publish two new books in 2023, one of which is already complete.

The evolution of an author takes time, but it can be a beautiful process. And for me, even the detours have made the journey worthwhile. If you're still starting out, I promise you it is worth the wait!

Anne Scottlin, MA, CPC, is a global impact strategist, award-winning author, actress and speaker. Her passion is powerfully supporting leaders and changemakers to make the world a better place. Scottlin's joy is to work with individuals and organizations who have a heart for humanity and a vision to make a global impact.

02

Pub Date: April 25, 2021
ISBN: 13: 978-1-94687-583-9
Book Category/Genre: Non-fiction/Health
Page Count: 286
Publisher: Self-Published

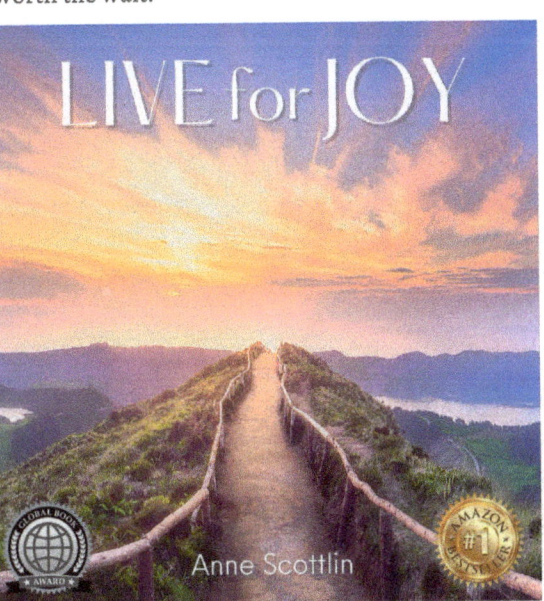

LIVE for JOY

Anne Scottlin

My Second Family: Confessions of a Sci-Fi Writer

Sher J. Stultz

As I climbed the castle stairs to my science lab, I stopped to look at Commencement Bay. It's a stunning view, and I never miss a chance to catch a glimpse. A colleague passed me on the landing and stopped to chat. She was delighted that I was writing a time travel adventure series and asked me about my process of developing characters that span generations. I hesitated to explain because I knew it would sound looney, but I couldn't think of anything authentic in its place.

People assume that because I'm a science teacher, I have some cleverly organized schema for character development. I use a spreadsheet to track birthdays, relationships, important events, and time travel abilities of the characters in my stories. Still, my brain diverges from the logical process people assume writers employ when developing characters. Because Cassie, Aeneas, Tabitha, C.J., Socrates, and Harold, to name a few, tag along with me all day.

"They're just in your head all the time?" she asked, incredulous.

I forced myself not to tear up because they're like my second family, and I feel silly explaining their existence.

"They go everywhere with me, and when I need them, they appear. I even talk with them."

She shook her head, laughing. As a teacher, you have enough to keep track of during the school day without adding a cast of characters to the mix.

In the early days when I was writing what would become The Rescue, Book One of The Timestream Travelers, I was cruising my favorite neighborhood in West Seattle, the setting for the series. West Seattle is an offshoot of the big city, a quirky haven of shops, parks, old craftsman houses, and stunning views of the Puget Sound. I fell in love with the place and spent hours walking the streets around Hiawatha Playfield. One day I was headed to Freshy's (a crowning jewel of a coffee shop) to do some writing when Tabitha strolled past me. I halted, turned, and couldn't believe my eyes. The long, wavy, auburn hair, the friendly smile, and the confident gait were just as I'd imagined her for years. Tabitha is a fictional character. I know that. But what are the odds her doppelganger would be in the neighborhood where she would live if she were a real person?

All writers are world builders; some build from scratch, and others build on existing foundations. Our brains are full of vivid imagery, adventurous storylines, idiosyncratic characters, and endless possibilities searching for outlets. So we write. And for many of us, the characters are just as real to us as your best friends are to you. Mine hang out with me at an iconic high school in downtown Tacoma waiting for me to write their stories when I get home.

Sher Stultz lives with her family in the Puyallup river valley. The Timestream Travelers Chronicles is her debut series. Her inspiration for these stories sprang from teaching middle school science and her deep curiosity about genetics and time travel. As a science teacher for seventeen years, she is always delighted to bump into former students and learn about the new adventures in their lives. She kayaks, dances, practices yoga, and goes camping or hiking in her spare time. In the summertime, Sher grows pollinator gardens for bees and hummingbirds, attends outdoor concerts, and reads in her hammock. An ardent conversationalist, Sher enjoys many genres of books and music and will happily converse with anyone on various topics!

Pub Date: January 10, 2022
ISBN: 13: 979-8-45544-054-0
Book Category/Genre: YA/ SCI-FI
Page Count: 290
Publisher: Self-Published

The Rescue
Book One of The Timestream Travelers Chronicles

By Sher J. Stultz

An Author Story
Gary Robinson

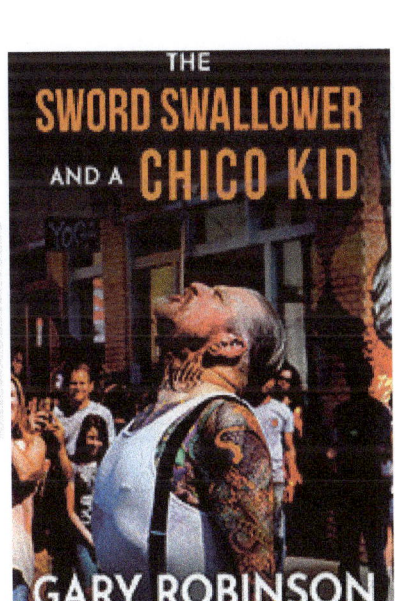

I originally started writing my first book as a cathartic exercise to help with the grief from my divorce. I always wanted to author stories, but with the long hours associated with my career, raising three South American kids, and fostering a relationship with my wife, I found my available time consumed with these blessings.

When I finally made that leap to become a writer, and my kids and family were no longer in my daily life, I would allocate my evenings to drafting my first book. I would spend my commutes thinking of funny but poignant phrases to add to the present narrative I was working on that day.

So much of life has happened to me since I finished "The Sword Swallower and a Chico Kid" five years ago. I nearly died twice from lung cancer and battled a life-threatening liver infection. I left my job of twenty years and soon lost another job to Covid. I spent a summer with my ailing father and accepted another career in an unfamiliar town. My first job was managed by a narcissist, which compelled me to wake up at 3:00 am and write with great urgency in coffee shops, abandoned parking lots, lunch breaks, evenings, or any opportunity I could find to develop my story.

My second book, which has not yet been published but is completed, was a testament to perseverance. I produced six drafts, went through three editors, paid for development critiquing, and spent many days refining and reimagining my story.

I believe I have produced a great piece of work. The story is called "The Wayward Son," I am looking forward to introducing this book to the Online Book Club membership.

Gary is a new author and intends to devote a good part of his life to writing stories about how he views the world around him. He hopes to find the stories compelling, thought-provoking and entertaining. His friendship inspired the Sword Swallower and a Chico Kid with a retired circus sideshow sword swallower. He is working on his next book and will announce the release date as soon as he finishes the first draft.

Pub Date: September 26, 2017
ISBN: 13: 978-0-99946-980-4
Book Category/Genre: Fiction
Page Count: 302
Publisher: Grobinbooks

Finding Freedom and Truth in A Reservoir Man

L.J. Ambrosio

Michael's truth in "A Reservoir Man" is not about academic truth but a personal spiritual reality. His journey from childhood to the end of the novel slowly uncovers who he is, avoiding the corruption of the Reservoir Man. Michael does not view the Reservoir Man as the instrument of corruption but as the carrier of the corruption virus. As he peels away all the restrictions in his life, he comes closer to his own personal and spiritual freedom.

Michael does not understand why these Reservoir Men attempt to take advantage of him and infect him with their corruption. Michael searches for what it is inside of himself that attracts these people towards him. In order to not distract from his quest, Michael does not fight these Reservoir Men. Instead, he listens to their life stories, takes their lessons, and moves on. He grows in his insight and spiritual strength towards the light of his freedom with every encounter he survives.

In the novel, only a few Reservoir Men truly stump him, delay his growth, and take advantage of him. One of the two most dangerous Reservoir Men in the novel is the Dean of his Graduate school; the other is his business partner. He is fooled because he trusts them, and they are falsely masked.

As his journey continues, he unlocks the chains that have been blinding his truth; Michael can clearly see his universe and the beauty around him as he continues his walk through time. He understands the pain and agony of the Reservoir Men and the importance of his escape from them. Michael's final metaphor in the novel is a river of change. The river represents time and how one can stand at the riverbank and never see the same exact water flowing twice. In the same way, the river flows, Michael's journey always moves forward towards his inevitable truth. He is free of the Reservoir Man; he has found his freedom. He never repeats a part of the journey or looks back. In the end, it was the journey to find his truth that gave Michael his freedom.

Louis J. Ambrosio ran one of the most nurturing bi-coastal talent agencies in Los Angeles and New York. He started his career as a theatrical producer, running two major regional theatres for eight seasons. During his impressive career, Ambrosio also distinguished himself as an award-winning film producer and novelist. He also taught at over seven major Universities.

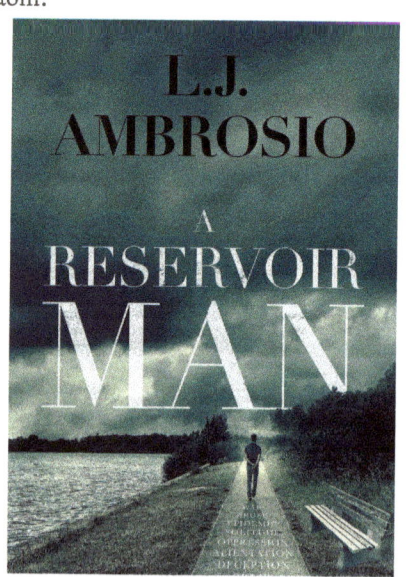

Pub Date: June 18, 2022
ISBN: 13: 979-8-98596-511-7
Book Category/Genre: Memoir
Page Count: 340
Publisher: Film Valor

05

Childhood Inspiration Begets Hollywood Homage

Anna J Stewart

After publishing more than fifty romances, it's challenging to think of the inspiration behind each book. I remember some immediately, others take more work, and others still don't know. I often barely recall writing the stories at all, mainly because I'm usually already thinking about and moving on to the next one. But with EXPOSED, my November romantic suspense release from ArcManor's Caezik Romance, I can tell you exactly where the inspiration came from. My childhood.

I'm a self-admitted child of the 70s. I was raised in San Francisco, in the Sunset district. I was a reasonably active kid—I had a bike, I gave skateboarding an enthusiastic try, and I was stellar on roller skates. But what I really excelled at was watching TV. These were pre-VCR days when television stations (I think we had six to choose from?) offered a much wider variety of programming than they do now.

Saturday morning cartoons were appointment television, and the afternoons were filled with Shirley Temple, Abbot and Costello, and Errol Flynn movies. I knew who Bogie and Bacall were from when I could walk. When I discovered the magic that was Marilyn Monroe (we actually share a birthday), my fascination with Old Hollywood was locked, and my life-long obsession was triggered.

When I was sixteen, a trip to one of my local bookstores led me to the biography section, and there I found the most amazing book: a collection of Hollywood studio portraits of all the mega-stars of their day. Bogart, Flynn, Monroe, to be sure. But also Jane Russell, Bette Davis, Joan Crawford, and many more. Joan Fontaine? Still my favorite Jane Eyre. I loved that book so much that I nearly broke the binding. I looked at it so many times. So, my Arc Manor editor Lezli proposed I write a full-length romance for them by asking, "What do you want to write?" I immediately thought of a thread of an idea I'd been pulling out for a while. That thread began with the all-important question: What if?

What if... a photographer came across some old film that, when developed, was evidence of a murder no one knew had happened.

This entire question came about after watching an episode of White Collar, where Mozzie (a secondary character) bids on and wins an old storage unit filled with cameras and film (and a bunch of other junk). But the cameras...oh, that's what got me. With my editor's question ringing, I knew I needed to answer my 'what if?' And so, EXPOSED, the first in my Circle of the Red Lily books, was born. Part of me will always long for those days of old when Hollywood evoked a mystique that was tightly controlled albeit magnificently projected.

Instead, for the following few books, I'll get to play and imagine and add in my own twists and turns of the Golden Age, intertwine a healthy dose of mystery, murder, danger and mayhem, and of course, a delicious hero who sweeps a feisty heroine off her feet. From this writer's perspective? It doesn't get much better than that.

Anna loves writing big community stories where family is always the theme. Since her first published novella with Harlequin in 2014, Anna has released more than fifty novels and novellas and hopes to branch out even more. Anna lives in Northern California, where (at the best times) she loves going to the movies, attending fan conventions, and heading to Disneyland, her favorite place on earth.

Pub Date: November 15, 2022
ISBN: 13: 978-1-64710-067-4
Book Category/Genre: Action Adventure
Page Count: 200
Publisher: CAEZIK Romance

06

Sally's Sensational Sense of Smell
Chris Lau

When did you first realize you wanted to be a writer?

Quite late on in my life, actually. I have always loved reading and greatly admired writers, but I never once thought of being a writer. However, I always have story ideas in my head that I would think about to help me go to sleep. I would make up a different ending to films or books I disagreed with. One day, I decided to write down these thoughts, and when I started, I couldn't stop. The stories seemed to take on a life of their own, and I kept writing.

How do you schedule your life when you're writing?

I am an early riser, so I tend to schedule writing in the morning when the house is quiet, and I haven't filled my head with other thoughts yet.

What would you say is your interesting writing quirk?

I like writing stories with a twist, so I know how I want it to end, and I have to write the story backwards. I start with the ending and then write the plot around that to build the story towards the ending.

Where did you get your information or idea for your book?

I was chatting to some mums about our children and their funny conversations. I liked one of them and thought it would be an excellent idea for a book character and story.

What do you like to do when you're not writing?

Read! I love reading, and my dream would be to have a huge library or own a little bookstore where I can sit in the corner and read. I also love to bake.

Chris is a Scottish-Chinese writer and a busy working mum. She is a Financial Services honours graduate and has worked in the financial planning industry for over 18 years.

Chris has always had a passion for writing and started writing scripts in the horror comedy genre to amuse herself and others. She won a place in 2019 doing a writing workshop on Write Lines with In Motion Theatre Company in Association with Glasgow Libraries.

Sally's Sensational Sense of Smell is her debut children's book, and it developed from an idea at a mum's coffee morning with Jo. Both of their children started primary school in the same class.

Pub Date: November 25, 2021
ISBN: 13: 978-1-73985-692-2
Book Category/Genre:
Children's Book
Page Count: 38
Publisher: Rowan Archer

07

Sally's Sensational Sense of Smell

Written by
CHRIS LAU

Illustrated by
JO ADAM

Ghost Mark
JP McLean

What would you say is your interesting writing quirk?

I've developed a separation of workstations depending on what type of writing I'm doing. I have no idea how this came about. There are two places where I work. One is a corner in the dining room with a comfortable chair with a view of the ocean. It's there that I am at my most creative, so most of my novel writing happens there. I also have a chair in the living room where I tend to the business side of writing. Oddly enough, I rarely use the office at the back of the house. It has a "work" vibe and no view.

Where did you get your information or idea for your book?

The idea was sparked by an NBC series called Blind Spot, which starred Jaimie Alexander. The first episode's opening scene shows a bomb squad tech approaching an abandoned duffle bag in an empty Times Square. Emerging from the bag is a woman covered in tattoos from the neck down. The woman doesn't remember who she is or how she got the ink. When I first saw that woman with tattoos, it stirred my imagination. I wondered what it might be like to live with markings that weren't your choice. That was the seed for Blood Mark, and I developed it from there.

What do you like to do when you're not writing?

I love gardening and taking walks in the forest or along the ocean. My gardens used to be pristine, but writing has eaten into the time to weed, so I'm learning to ignore the odd unwanted "flower" and live with imperfection. As for the walks, they're a necessity. My back reminds me that I need to get active when I put off physical exercise for too long. A bonus of the walks is that I get some beautiful photos to share on social media.

What was one of the most surprising things you learned in creating your book?

I never thought I'd have an idea big enough for a book, but I've since learned that you don't need a single BIG idea. Sometimes, starting with a smaller idea is a fine place to begin. I started my first book that way, writing just one scene. Writing that scene prompted me to think about what came before it and what followed. Soon, that scene grew into two, ten, and then a book. In the end, I had seven books in that series.

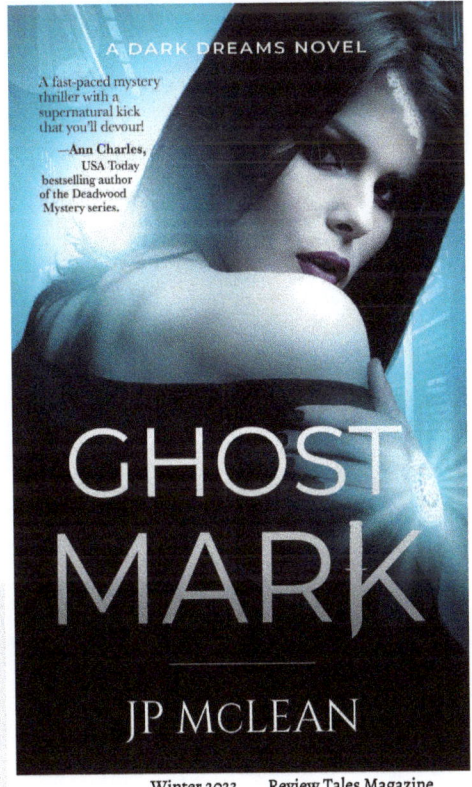

A DARK DREAMS NOVEL

A fast-paced mystery thriller with a supernatural kick that you'll devour!

—**Ann Charles**, USA Today bestselling author of the Deadwood Mystery series.

GHOST MARK

JP MCLEAN

JP (Jo-Anne) McLean is a bestselling author of urban fantasy and supernatural thrillers. She is a Global Book Award winner, a CIBA and Page Turner Award finalist, received the Reader's House Editor's Choice Award of Excellence, and has received honours from the Eric Hoffer Book Awards, the Wishing Shelf Book Awards, the NIEA Awards, and the Whistler Independent Book Awards. She lives on Canada's west coast.

Pub Date: November 1, 2022
ISBN: 13: 978-1-98812-563-3
Book Category/Genre: Supernatural Thriller
Page Count: 284
Publisher: WindStorm Press

08

Winter Pale
Marina Koulouri

When did you first realize you wanted to be a writer?

Like most children, I enjoyed stories very much. I was always absorbed by a good story, and I would often act it out and create my own version of it. As a teenager, I started writing short stories, hiding them somewhere so that no one would find and read them. They were my secret treasure, a getaway only I had access to. But I didn't realize I wanted to be a writer until several decades later when a compelling need emerged: the need to communicate these stories to an audience.

How do you schedule your life when you're writing?

With a job and family, finding time for writing takes much coordination. I devote every hour of my free time to writing, and I often stay up late or wake up really early in the morning to catch up with it. I mostly write at the expense of my rest and sleep. People around me often complain when I'm in my writing phase because I become a hermit, but that's the way it has to be. Because writing is not just a hobby or even a passion for me; it defines who I am.

How did you get your book published?

My first two books in Greek were traditionally published, but, going for the international market with my debut English novel, self-publishing seemed inevitable. More and more authors now go for self-publication, and many publications are of high professional standards. Yes, I believe self-publishing is no more as tainted as it used to be. And it gives the author much freedom of choice and the opportunity to personalize how the book is communicated. This brings authors and readers closer together, and it's wonderful. The process is overwhelming at times, but it is also very creative.

Is there anything you would like to confess about as an author?

This experience with a beta reader gave me the feeling that I must be doing something right! You see, I write with the basic outline always in mind, but many of the details in the plot really come instinctively, without much thought. Then this reader came up to me and said, "The way you had your protagonist lose her identity card as a means to say she was about to start discovering a new self, that was brilliant!" I said thank you, of course, but I was really dumbfounded and wondered, "Did I really do that?"

Marina Koulouri writes Historical Fiction and Historical Romance, featuring strong emotional histories with a moral dilemmas leading her characters to discover a painful yet enlightening and liberating truth about themselves. Born and raised in the largest port city in Greece, she has learnt to appreciate diversity and distinguish the mainly human attributes in people from different backgrounds, a powerful uniting force. When she is not writing, she teaches English as a foreign language.

Pub Date: November 28, 2022
ISBN: 13: 978-6-18862-420-7
Book Category/Genre:
Historical Romance
Page Count: 340
Publisher: Self-Published

The Interstellar Police Force, Book One: The Historic Mission
Raymond F. Klein

When did you first realize you wanted to be a writer?

Well, it was something I never really thought about until 2006. I am a big fan of the original Twilight Zone TV series, and I was attempting to update one of the episodes in the hopes of writing a modernized screenplay and making it into an Indy film. What I wound up with was a short novel. I had no idea about copyright laws, so I put it aside. But thought that this was something I could do. About three months later, the original idea for my novel, The Interstellar Police Force, Book One: The Historic Mission, came to me, which I completed in 2013.

Where did you get your information or idea for your book?

Well, this may be a little odd, but here we go. I was driving home one day while listening to the radio. At a stop light, the song "Smack My Bitch Up" from the English electronic punk band The Prodigy came on. And as it was playing, I imagined a 1959 Ford Thunderbird coming out of the sky and landing in the lane next to me. A guy in dark glasses was driving, and sitting next to him in the passenger's seat was a Doberman Pincher. Yeah, I know! Crazy how the brain works.

What was one of the most surprising things you learned in creating your book?

One of the things that surprised me the most about writing this was how some events unfolded on their own. Several paragraphs just flooded onto the pages on their own accord. Without me pre-writing it or even thinking about it beforehand. Like I was watching the outcome of a movie playing in my head. That, I thought, was a pretty cool process.

What do you like to do when you're not writing?

When not writing, I'm reading or just watching TV. Some authors I gravitate toward are Dean Knootz, Jeffery Deaver, Dennis Lahane and Stephen King, and many others. Regarding TV, I like anthology type of series like The Twilight Zone and Netflix's Black Mirror. Along with streaming comedies and dramas. And, of course, one of my all-time favorite Sci-Fi shows, the short-lived space drama Firefly.

Raymond is a first-time author and lives in Wesley Chapel, Florida, thirty minutes north of Tampa. He works for the ABC-TV affiliate WFTS and has been in the television industry off and on for about twenty years.

Pub Date: March 13, 2021
ISBN: 13: 979-8-72158-192-2
Book Category/Genre: Science Fiction
Page Count: 292
Publisher: Self-Published

Christmas on Rosy Lane
Rose Elaine

When did you first realize you wanted to be a writer?

I failed 10th-grade English. My teacher was an editor, and I was very creative. I used poetic license with everything from spelling, grammar and how to construct a narrative. My English teacher disapproved. I retook English that summer, and a different teacher told me I had a voice. She encouraged my writing. She asked me to write more. That same year I sent an article to a teen magazine, confident they would publish my work. My story wasn't published, but I could write for the first time and have been writing ever since.

How do you schedule your life when you're writing?

Creating Rosy Lane the books and artwork is a full-time job. I begin working by 9:00 am every morning, Monday through Friday, and work until 5:00 pm. I manage every aspect of the process. I have a routine but allow myself to go with the flow. Writing and painting are creative pursuits, and when I am inspired, I follow the muse. I have had to discipline myself to do less creative things, manage a business, and think about the bottom line. When I focus on what is essential now – everything falls into place.

What would you say is your interesting writing quirk?

When I am writing or genuinely focused, I talk to myself. I say things out loud, like, "Wait, that won't work." – "Now, where was I?" "Hang on, I think I just used that," or "Wasn't that on..." and so forth. I often read what I wrote out loud to hear what I have said and give me perspective.

Where did you get your information or idea for your book?

My life has been filled with many experiences. I have been exposed to incredible sights, sounds, tastes, and lifestyles, and each brings me a greater understanding of the people and world in which we live. My stories and books are adaptations of these places and the people I have known. My mom and dad, my husband, my family, my friends, and the various locations I have lived in inspired me. I find such joy in finding connections between these different facets and creating a fictional world they can all call home.

Rose Elaine spins beauty out of pain, giving hope and joy to women worldwide who need a reprieve from their daily lives. Passionate about self-love and community, Rose Elaine inspires tenderness and self-care by creating her line of Rosy Lane-inspired teas, coffees, body scrubs, and lotions for busy women who deserve to pamper themselves. When she's not writing or creating her luxury goods, she lives an entire, heartwarming life with her husband, adult children, eleven cats, and her stunning watercolor paintings.

Pub Date: Jan 11, 2022
ISBN: 13: 978-1-95116-562-8
Book Category/Genre: Holiday Fiction
Page Count: 118
Publisher: Rose Elaine LLC

The Forty-Something Fanboy: A Midlife Crisis in the Age of COVID
Sam Choi

How do you schedule your life when you're writing?

My schedule for writing this book was a response to the early pandemic ... and I don't think it is repeatable. I used to travel nearly every week for work. When the COVID pandemic first hit and shut down many businesses, and certainly shut down travel, I suddenly had many extra hours in the day that I would have spent commuting or traveling. So I wrote for about an hour or two before work and an hour or two after work. Also, my wife decided to go to Korea during this time because she was not working, and the situation was much more controlled there. So I had nothing to do in the evenings or weekends, so I wrote then. There were some weeks I could write for more than 40 hours because of this. Now that businesses and our lives have adapted to COVID, I see this is the first opportunity around for a while.

Where did you get your information or idea for your book?

In the early days of the pandemic, I heard an NPR story about how isolation affected people. It focused on extroverts. I thought to myself how isolation might affect introverts. While introverts might not thrive at large parties, we still need social interaction. So I started to create the situation for my protagonist, imagining how isolated he could be. I started with him being single, but then quickly changed him to being divorced so that I could use the loss of that relationship as a driver in the story. Other elements, such as not being able to date, not being able to see his daughter, and not being able to enjoy activities with his few close friends, helped create the situation and generate ideas for conflicts and scenes for the story.

How do you process and deal with negative book reviews?

It is painful. I have to admit it. But I try to figure out what part of the story or the storytelling the person did not like. I'm not able to change it now, but I use it to try and understand different things people are reading.

Is there anything you would like to confess about as an author?

This experience has made me accept that as much as I imagine myself as a private person, I have an exhibitionist streak. Why else would I delight in publishing it for anyone worldwide to see? It's not me, but there are many elements of me in this story. I confess. I guess I'm a closet exhibitionist.

Sam Choi is an author, once academic, now corporate executive, father, and husband living in California, with one dog, two living parents, three email addresses, and dozens of defunct social media profiles.

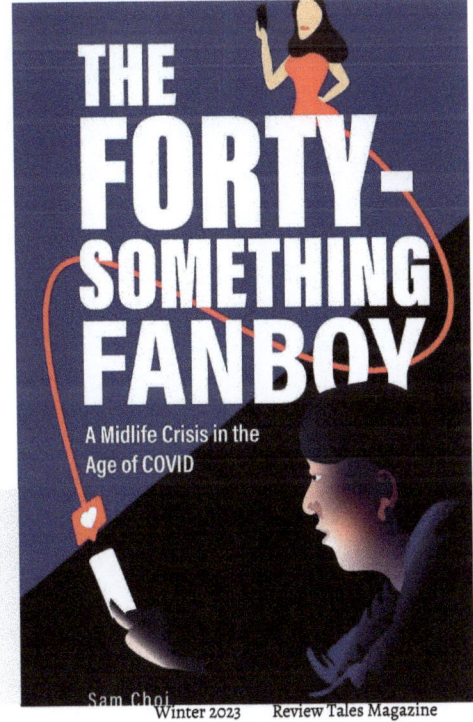

Pub Date: May 27, 2022
ISBN: 13: 978-1-00606-643-6
Book Category/Genre:
Contemporary Fiction
Page Count: 270
Publisher: Blurb

The First State
Tshekedi Wallace

When did you first realise you wanted to become a writer?

I was twelve years old when I came across The Hardy Boy's book, and I wanted to make other people get enjoyment from my ideas as much as they would from reading those books. Then I got into sci-fi. First, it was War Of The Worlds and Dune. Then I got hooked on sci-fi movies with a comic book style like Demolition Man. My plan has always been to write books that catapult the reader into a world where they can really escape from their real lives.

Where did you get your information or idea for your book?

I see a vision in my mind to get my own ideas. It is hard to come up with fresh ideas, but usually, I start by coming up with decent character profiles that will heavily affect the story structure. If I read books and see strong character development, it really helps me think about how I will strengthen my own work. For The First State, I looked into the history of oppressed states and dictatorships in real life and fictional stories. I used my imagination to create a horrible tyrant that needs to be defeated.

What was one of the most surprising things you learned in creating your book?

I was surprised that I could cut myself away from the things I love to do so systematically. I missed many things, like watching a series I had never missed before and going out to meet people I never turned down when they called. I didn't become a hermit, but things have changed. Over the years, writing has become a major part of my whole life, and this book took much time to get right. I gave up a lot of time and energy and never got tired of doing it or regretted it.

What would you say is your interesting writing quirk?

I wouldn't call it too much of a quirk, but I am a stickler for making chapter notes. I have them all over the place on the notes section of my iPhone, and I'll fill up notepads. I can change things on the chapter notes like crazy. I love making points and seeing if I can do better than before when I go over the notes. It is my madness as well. I chuckle about it sometimes.

Tshekedi Wallace is named after Tshekedi the Great, the King of the Bamangwato of Botswana. In keeping with his namesake, Tshekedi Wallace, born in Leeds, is a committed advocate for freedom due to his upbringing. He was born into a well-known family of struggle heroes who fought for the liberation of their people. He grew up listening to vigorous debates about politics, history, and issues of the day mainly discussed at the dinner table. This has given him an enduring love for history, literature, art, and politics. In his spare time, he writes poetry.

The First State
Tshekedi Wallace

Pub Date: August 19, 2022
ISBN: 13: 978-1-98868-018-7
Book Category/Genre: Science Fiction
Page Count: 237
Publisher: Review Tales Publishing & Editing Services

1 2 3 Count with Me on Granddad's Farm
Valerie D. Johnson

When did you first realize you wanted to be a writer?

I've always enjoyed writing stories and poems in elementary school. Also, I enjoyed sharing and interactive writing with my students as a classroom teacher. However, I just knew I wanted to share my love of math with the world, and writing would be a way to do it.

During my tenure as a classroom teacher, I noticed that students often exhibited math anxiety or expressed how much they disliked math. Truth be told, I never thought of myself as a "math person." Math was not my favorite subject as a student; it was too abstract. But now that I'm a mathematics specialist, I not only know the how, but I also understand the why. Now, I LOVE MATH, and my mission is to ignite a love of math in all children, one book at a time.

What would you say is your interesting writing quirk?

First, I do a brain dump on a Word doc of my proposed titles, characters, and setting. Then, I take several field trips to bookstores to look at, touch and read picture books. I note the different elements (i.e. title, setting, theme, etc.) of new releases and #1 best sellers. Now, I can sit down and write (actually type) my first draft.

While writing or editing, I constantly save my work. I keep a copy on two flash drives and one on my desktop. I research facts throughout the entire process and add or delete them as I rewrite each draft.

Where did you get your information or idea for your book?

This story was inspired by summers on my grandfather's farm. The concept of the book is based on my work with mathematicians in grades K-6 as an Elementary Math Resource Teacher. And I dedicated this book to my Aunt Katherine Johnson, NASA Mathematician and Hidden Figure because she loved to count.

Valerie D. Johnson is an educator, speaker, and author of 1 2 3 Count with Me on Granddad's Farm. 1 2 3 Count with Me on Granddad's Farm is a heartwarming and visually-engaging picture book showing the love and everlasting bond between grandchildren and grandparents while teaching young readers to count to 10. Valerie's superpower is making learning math easy to understand, engaging, meaningful, and fun. Her mission is to ignite a love of math in all children, one book at a time!

Pub Date: August 30, 2022
ISBN: 13: 979-8-98630-780-0
Book Category/Genre: Children's Book
Page Count: 32
Publisher: West Oak Lane Kids, LLC

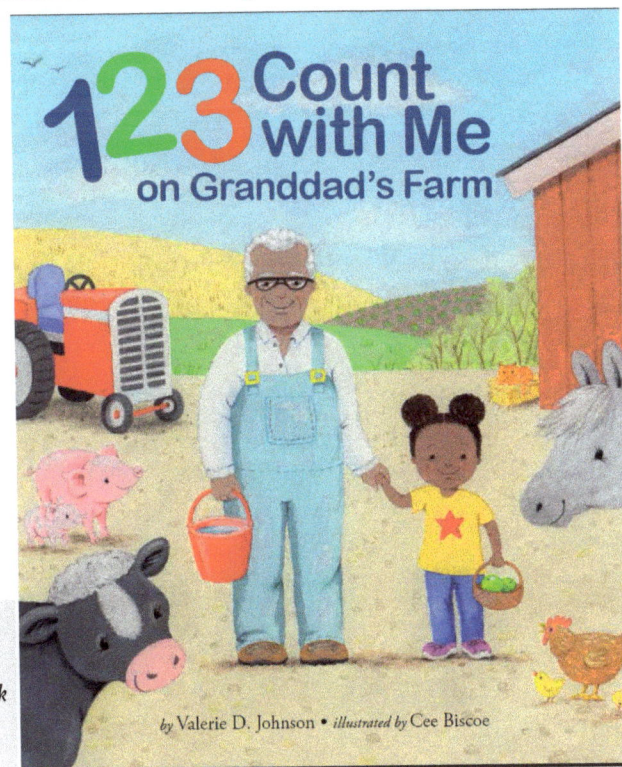

by Valerie D. Johnson • illustrated by Cee Biscoe

14

**Final Notice
Van Fleisher**

What do you like to do when you're not writing?

I like to stay busy. I'm still in a management consulting partnership and on two non-profit boards, one of which I'm the CEO. I started a group to create public spaces for off-leash dog activities. It's been successful, so I'm at the dog park daily. And that's why there's always a dog in my books.

What was one of the most surprising things you learned in creating your book?

How easy it was to write and publish and how hard it was to market.

Is there anything you would like to confess about as an author?

I've already confessed to being a comma-dunce. And then, there's this funny story. In my senior year in high school, my English teacher asked what books I read. My answer of "None" surprised him, and he handed me a copy of "Catcher in the Rye." I was jock and assumed he'd given me the book in recognition of that. I read through the book with great enjoyment and a vain search for the baseball part that was indeed there. I became an avid reader.

As a child, what did you want to do when you grew up?

Become a baseball or football star.

How do you process and deal with negative book reviews?

It bothered me at first, but the relatively few negative reviews pale compared to the long-lasting glow of the good ones. I am really moved when someone writes that my book "changed the way" they look at things or it "really made me think."

During his first two careers – one with an airline and the other in management consulting- Van lived on planes and in airports. The only healthy antidote to the terminal and in-flight boredom was reading, so he read every thriller in the airport bookstores.
Van retired at 73, and when he woke up on his first retirement day, he hadn't a clue what to do. So, he figured that if Clancy and Patterson could do it, so could he.

15

Pub Date: January 23, 2018
ISBN: 13: 978-1-73208-330-1
Book Category/Genre: Political Thriller
Page Count: 343
Publisher: VF3

The Tangled Stars
Edward Willett

When did you first realize you wanted to be a writer?

When I was eleven, a friend and I filled a rainy afternoon (in those halcyon pre-Internet days) by writing short stories. I don't think he ever finished his, but I finished mine. It was called "Kastra Glazz: Hypership Test Pilot" (a solid indication my future as a science fiction writer was already in the cards), and after my mother typed it up for me, my junior high English teacher, Tony Tunbridge, did me the honour of properly critiquing it, rather than just patting me on the head for having written it. I've credited him ever since with lighting a little fire under me that encouraged me to improve the next thing I wrote. I think that's when I knew writing would be part of my life, but it all began with reading. I decided to be a writer because I wanted to tell stories to other people they would enjoy as much as I enjoyed the work of the writers I read growing up.

How do you schedule your life when you're writing?

I've been a full-time freelance writer and editor for three decades now; I still don't schedule my life when I'm writing. I just try to put in some time on whatever the project is as I can, working around other deadlines and demands on my time (freelance editing jobs, running my publishing company, etc.). It's very unstructured, but eventually, things get written. When I focus on it, I can write a 100,000-word novel in a month; I've done a 60,000-word YA novel in two weeks, and I once did 50,000 words of a novel in a single week. But it's generally more scattershot than that.

What do you like to do when you're not writing?

I'm a singer, actor, and writer, so I often rehearse something or other. I've performed in numerous plays, musicals, and operas, both just for fun and professionally, and sung in numerous high-end choirs, including the Canadian Chamber Choir and, currently, a self-directed choir called Wascana Voices.

Edward Willett is the award-winning author of more than sixty books of science fiction, fantasy, and non-fiction for readers of all ages, including The Tangled Stars, the Worldshapers series, and the Masks of Agyrima trilogy (as E.C. Blake) for DAW Books and the YA fantasy series The Shards of Excalibur, originally published by Coteau Books.

Pub Date: October 18, 2022
ISBN: 13: 978-0-75641-815-1
Book Category/Genre: Science Finction
Page Count: 420
Publisher: DAW Books

Words of Wisdom

VISUAL IMAGINATION IN WRITING

Charles Townsend

I have always had a strong visual imagination. When I was at school, I was good at art and hoped to win the school art prize, but it went to a kid in the year below. I have always been honest with myself, and his work did look better than mine. However, I believed my work was more imaginative, even though I was less good at translating the images I imagined onto paper. Not winning the art prize finished any thoughts I had of becoming an artist since if I were not the best artist in the school, I would certainly not be a top artist in the wider world. The kid who beat me went on to become an artist. His name is Anthony Gormley. Now Sir Anthony Gormley, the world-renowned artist.

My next thought was to use my visual imagination to be a film director. In my final year at university, I was about to apply for film school when I was offered a job in the industry. The lure of earning money was too strong, and I spent the next forty years in the industry and running companies. I was a tutor at a management training school for part of that time. One of the other tutors used to say that to make something memorable; you should use your words to form a picture in people's minds. This advice stuck with me, and I have used it ever since. In my writing, I visualise the action unfolding like a film script and describe what I see to the readers. If the characters are strong, they will act out their parts, and the whole will gain momentum. This works well for me. So, my advice to other writers is to use your imagination to envision and describe the situation. By doing this, your readers will also visualise it to become memorable.

Charles Townsend is a Member of The Magic Circle and enjoys devising new magic tricks. He is now retired from a long career running companies. He has pursued many interests over the years. He was a council member of the governing body of the sport of croquet, he has held a one-person art exhibition and loved antiques and history. In 2012 he took over a pub with his eldest son and built a brewery and distillery in the pub outbuildings. He lives with his wife Hayley in a historic house in old Harwich and has five children.

Pub Date: December 8, 2021
ISBN: 13: 978-1-91501-205-0
Book Category/Genre: Fantasy
Page Count: 348
Publisher: Self-Published

17

What's Your Inspiration?

George Pallas

In the noir film, The Maltese Falcon, Kasper Gutman (Sidney Greenstreet) tells private eye Sam Spade (Humphrey Bogart), "Talking's something you can't do judiciously unless you keep in practice." You could say the same, of course, about writing. Writing isn't something you can do well unless you write regularly. Sci-fi icon Ray Bradbury endorsed the same idea when he advised authors, "Write a short story every week. It's not possible to write 52 bad short stories in a row." Great advice, right? But what do you write about?

Choosing a subject and plot for a story has bedeviled authors since the invention of the written word. But finding the core of an idea doesn't have to be impossible. Like writing, generating ideas is something that comes easier with practice. And while you are developing your storytelling skills, there are ways to prime the pump, so to speak.

One of the easiest ways to develop ideas is to subscribe to a writing prompt. A simple Web search will bring up dozens of sites offering writing prompts. Some websites present static lists, while others send regular emails with ideas for starting or ending a story. Only some suggestions are gems, but many are clever with the potential to spur unique and fascinating tales.

If you're more of a do-it-yourself person, there are other ways to generate ideas. Sometimes, you need to look no further than incidents and anecdotes from your own life. With some dressing up, almost any seemingly mundane incident can become the basis for a piece. For example, when my sister complained about one of her cats getting stuck on her roof, I turned the incident into a short story, Bad Kitty.

As you write more, your ability to create characters and plots will develop to the point where almost anything can serve as a writing prompt. Even inanimate objects can anchor your work. Animals and pets also make good subjects because most people like animal stories (hence, Bad Kitty). Strangers you meet in public might give rise to a story about their secret lives or unusual abilities.

A little inspiration from these sources can kickstart your writing journey. With practice, coming up with characters and plots won't seem so hard.

Metamorphosis: An Anthology is the work of Joe Graves, Devon Ortega, George Pallas, et al. The book includes a brief bio of each author.

Pub Date: November 1, 2022
ISBN: 13: 979-8-98701-740-1
Book Category/Genre: Fantasy / Poetry
Page Count: 264
Publisher: Ohio Writers Group

Late Bloomers
John Ingram Walker, MD

Age has nothing to do with success:

·Joanne Kathleen (J.K.) Rowling is a classic example. A mediocre student, a low-level employee, a divorcee with a dependent child and multiple book rejections, she kept writing. The release of the first volume of the Harry Potter series came when she was 32 years old.

·Tom Brady, an all-pro quarterback, was not recruited out of high school.

·Michael Jordan didn't make his high school basketball team when he was in the 10th grade.

·Ray Kroc was 52 years old when he initiated the McDonald's fast-food franchise.

·Colonel Sanders was 62 when he began the Kentucky Fried Chicken franchise.

·Grandma Moses, the folk artist, did not begin painting seriously until she was 78 years old.

Waiting for Acceptance:

·Only William Shakespeare has sold more compositors than Agatha Christie, but it took 5-years of continual rejections before she found a publisher.

·Louis L'Amour had 200 rejections until his first book was sold. Since then, L'Amour's books have sold more than 300 million copies worldwide.

·Chicken Soup for Your Soul received 140 rejections before selling well over 125 million copies

·Gone with the Wind was rejected 38 times before 30 million copies were sold

·The Help received 60 rejections

·The Notebook by Nicholas Sparks was rejected by 24 literary agencies, the 25th purchased the romance for 1 million

·John Grisham's A Time to Kill was rejected by 28 times before 250 million copies were sold

Thomas Edison wrote the following words of encouragement: "Our greatest weakness is giving up. The surest way to succeed is to try one more time.

If you feel your writing is unappreciated, or you think you are too old to begin, don't despair. Keep writing. Keep dreaming. Keep working. You will eventually discover the unique writing style that pleases you and captivates others.

Dr. Walker has written fifteen books. He is retired Clinical Professor of Psychiatry at the University of Texas Medical School, San Antonio. He and his wife have two children and four grandchildren. They enjoy riding their horses Thunder and Lightning on their Flying W Ranch in Navasota, Texas.

Pub Date: August 20, 2021
ISBN: 13: 978-1-95281-665-9
Book Category/Genre:
Historical Fiction
Page Count: 175
Publisher: TouchPoint Press

THE MAGICIAN'S SECRET
Charles Townsend

'The Magician's Secret' is a thriller about Delvin overcoming a tremendous ordeal of proving his innocence on a crime he never committed and a mysterious piece of treasure with magical properties that is wanted by all.

The novel is fast-paced, and you are instantly invited into Delvin's world. The descriptive nature of the storyline provides details and all the difficulties Delvin and his friend, Jarla, face trying to create peace in the lands.

The connection between Delvin and his friend was exceptionally delightful. It added a certain dynamic to the story, which induced more excitement and enchantment. I appreciated how Jarla brought certain characteristics out of Delvin, making him more relatable and likeable.

The author's style of writing and the way the scenes were presented was entertaining. If you are into science fiction and enjoy drama, action, adventure and magic, this book is for you.

Reviewed by Jeyran Main

20

BRANDY, BALLAD OF A PIRATE PRINCESS

Dan E. Hendrickson

'Brandy, Ballad of a Pirate Princess,' is a historical fiction about Brandy, raised by pirates. When Dom Lomoche kills Brady's father and her mother's secret is revealed, Brady has to lift the curse from the ship and claim her right in this world.

The story was highly descriptive and filled with a beautiful narrative on the Caribbean islands. The battles and the way the storyline and the scenes interacted were exceptional. Everything from the characters and how they were developed created an enticing story.

The cover design complemented the content inside. The steady pace kept the reader wanting more, and as it was a historical novel, the facts and timing of things were well-researched and put together.

What predominately stood out in this book was Brandy herself. Her personality and demeanour towards everything were admirable, and how she dealt with all that was against her was a delight.

I recommend this book to fiction readers and those who like stories that contain thrilling concepts.

Reviewed by Jeyran Main

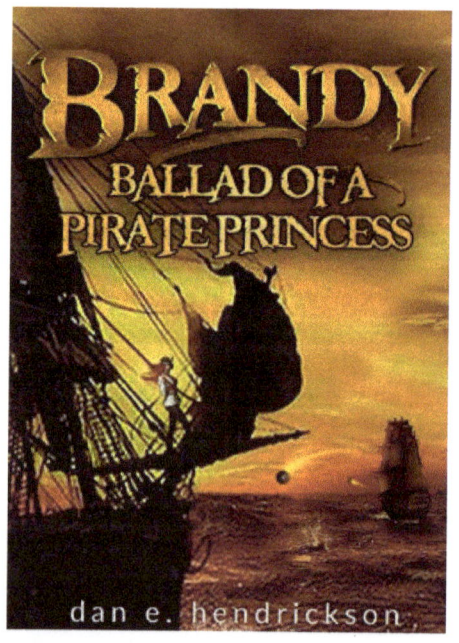

24

MARK VICTOR HANSEN, RELENTLESS: WISDOM BEHIND THE INCOMPARABLE CHICKEN SOUP FOR THE SOUL

Mitzi Perdue

'Mark Victor Hansen, Relentless' is a non-fiction book and an educational biography about being strong, impactful and how to succeed with a resilient work ethic and a relentless spirit.

The book is written well, but above all, it is inspirational. The literature has an easy flow to it. It is organised and, although it is not short, still remains intriguing and informative.

The added humour is a bonus and keeps the material upbeat. If you are attempting to reach your full potential and enrich your life, then you will find this book to be useful. The whole content is organised and to the point; you also get to understand the concept of the premise and learn a thing or two.

Each chapter displays an honest account of what the author has inherited as an inspirational educator. The most important aspect of the book is that it makes you feel as if you, too, can pursue your dream.

I recommend this book to self-help readers and non-fiction readers.

Reviewed by Jeyran Main

IN IT TOGETHER: THE BEAUTIFUL STRUGGLE UNITING US ALL

Eckhart Aurelius Hughes

'In It Together' is a non-fiction self-help book about happiness, self-discipline and emotions that can be overwhelming at times but also empowering.

The book provides a window for its audience and presents the concept of loving yourself while you associate it with multiple platforms of realities you face. Some of these realities are sad and could drain much of your energy. They can scar your soul and induce much self-criticism. The author provides a certain mindset to have its reader overcome these trains of thought.

It is clear to see that the intent here is to provide an insightful and useful tool for gaining inner peace. Some may not agree with all that is being said, but what does stand here is a different perspective, so I appreciated this book.

The literature is written well. The content is organized and has a nice flow to it. It is a well-put-together book. I recommend this book to those who wish to make a difference in their lives and to self-help fans.

Reviewed by Jeyran Main

In It Together
Eckhart Aurelius Hughes

The Beautiful Struggle Uniting Us All

23

TEN RECOMMANDMENTS FOR PERSONAL EMPOWERMENT

Dana Sardano

'Ten Recommandments for Personal Empowerment' is a biography about how Dana grows up in a not-so-friendly environment and empowers herself through all the trauma to live happily and have a more successful life.

The content contains ten recommandments designed to empower readers to go back to their past and look at everything from a different perspective. It is all about healing and assisting the reader, so it is a useful self-help read.

The other important factor about this book is how it is written. The words are easy to follow and understand. It is written with honesty and methodically explains what triggers us as humans and how we overcome them.

What I predominately enjoyed about this work was its approach. While the content was informative and educational, it also presented a unique perspective. I recommend this book to those interested in self-healing and empowering books.

Reviewed by Jeyran Main

Editor's Pick

APOLLO'S RAVEN BY LINNEA TANNER

The world is in turmoil. Celtic kings hand-picked by Rome to rule are fighting each other for power. King Amren's former queen, a powerful druid, has cast a curse that foretells Blood Wolf and the Raven will rise and destroy him. When Roman envoys unexpectedly arrive with a cohort of legionaries and demand King Amren's fealty, his rule begins to implode.

TERMS OF SERVICE: SUBJECT TO CHANGE WITHOUT NOTICE BY CRAIG W. STANFILL

Start with 1984, add in a healthy dose of Brave New World and Fahrenheit 451, stir in a bit of The Matrix and Blade Runner, and you have Terms of Service. It is a thought-provoking exploration of the profound consequences to our society as the digital world and the all-powerful corporations who rule it play an ever-greater role in our lives and we all wonder, where does it end?

25

www.ingramcontent.com/pod-product-compliance
Lightning Source LLC
Chambersburg PA
CBHW041530120626
46551CB00018B/2637